PICKS!

THE PEOPLE'S CHOICE VS
GOD'S CHOICE

PICKS!

THE PEOPLE'S CHOICE VS GOD'S CHOICE

NORMA EVANS BARBER

Faces Of Persons Whom The People Picked Vs Persons Whom God Picked

ARPress

ILLUMINATING IDEAS
EMPOWERING VOICES

ARPress
45 Dan Road Suite 5
Canton, MA 02021

Hotline: 1(888) 821-0229
Fax: 1(508) 545-7580

Ordering Information:
Quantity sales. Special discounts are available on quantity purchases by corporations, associations, and others. For details, contact the publisher at the address above.

Printed in the United States of America.

ISBN-13:   Softcover   979-8-89356-863-9
                      eBook   979-8-89356-864-6

Library of Congress Control Number: 2024909004

TABLE OF CONTENTS

PICKS!

The People's Choice vs God's Choice

ABOUT THIS BOOK

In the position that you now hold or that you aspire to, are you the people's pick or God's pick? Here, a number of Bible characters provide salient illustrations of the differences between God's rubric for voting for people as opposed to how humans choose. May you find help as you read in discerning and copying God's way of picking your leaders or presenting yourself as a leader in accomplishing the task the Lord has put you here on earth to do.

FOREWORD

When I left my homeland of Guyana over fifty years ago, I never considered myself as picked by God. I was twenty-five years old, but I had three older siblings, anyone one of whom God could have picked. Now, looking back over the "three score and ten" plus years of my life, I can see a pattern that confirms for me that I was not chosen by chance, but by a loving and merciful God, who, like He did for Joseph, picked me to accomplish His purposes in the lives of many others--generations of people whom I could not in any way foresee that my choices, careers, failures, and successes would have affected. Life situations were what transformed my perspective. How else would you explain my survival being impaled at my throat on a crowbar as a toddler? My older sister's life was simultaneously spared from typhoid fever since taking me to the hospital motivated my parents to take her at the same time for successful treatment. I can recall two other times when I actively saved people's lives, one a man passed out at the wheel while scores of cars rolled by, ignoring him, and the other--two kids from a burning house. Was it Chance, or was I picked?

My parents have long gone. More recently, my two older sisters passed on to their eternal reward. Now I find myself reflecting how over the years Father picked me from a little brownie chasing chickens, pigs, and sheep in a village called Danielstown on the shores of the Atlantic down in South America, to a countrified student in Georgetown, the capital city, to a missionary teacher in the hinterland among the Akawaios of Phillipai, and Patamonas of Paramakatoi-- beautiful Amerindian tribes, to experiencing the civil disturbances in the capital of the United States in the late 60s through the 70s, to the scholarly halls of Howard University, the University of Maryland and Regent University, to years of teaching babies, youths and young adults with special needs, back to teaching regular students in public and Christian settings, and then to finally retire to the life of a writer. I realize today, more than ever that I was picked, like David, the shepherd boy, as the most unlikely to succeed.

In retrospect I ask myself, was I faithful enough in spite of my many deficiencies? Will I hear "Well done?" It is important for us not only to do well but also to be "good and faithful." From the picks we portray in this book, it must be noted that none of them, except our Lord Jesus, was perfect. That tells us that God often picks the most unlikely to succeed, but if we trust Him absolutely, our messes can be turned into blessings. Paul affirms that we can have that assurance by saying, "all things work together for good to those who love God, to those who are called unto His purpose" (Romans 8:28).

That is the purpose of this book--for the reader who is not at the end of life's journey to introspect if he or she is fulfilling God's purpose in life. Is your life matching up to the rubric that Father intended for you when He birthed you on planet earth? For many of us, the journey is almost over, but for countless others, there is still time to work on being "good and faithful." May the lives of God's picks inspire you to do all you can while there is still time in your favor. Blessings!

Keywords: the people's choice, God's choice, picked, an understanding heart, if I perish, the wrong choice, deposed queen, conspiracy, divine intervention, God's perfect Lamb

PART ONE: KING SAUL--PICKED FOR APPEARANCE

1 Samuel 8:4-9 King James Version (KJV)

⁴*Then all the elders of Israel gathered themselves together, and came to Samuel unto Ramah,* ⁵*And said unto him, Behold, thou art old, and thy sons walk not in thy ways: now make us a king to judge us like all the nations.* ⁶*But the thing displeased Samuel, when they said, Give us a king to judge us. And Samuel prayed unto the Lord.* ⁷*And the Lord said unto Samuel, Hearken unto the voice of the people in all that they say unto thee: for they have not rejected thee, but they have rejected me, that I should not reign over them.* ⁸*According to all the works which they have done since the day that I brought them up out of Egypt even unto this day, wherewith they have forsaken "me." and served other gods, so do they also unto thee* ⁹*Now, therefore, hear, harken unto their voice: howbeit yet protest solemnly unto them, and shew them the manner of the king that shall reign over them.*

Chapter One
Give Us a King Like Other Nations

Samuel, the priestly judge, had walked in the fear of God from boyhood. As a little fella, he had learned from Eli, his priest guardian, and mentor, how to discern and hear God's voice. He grew up watching his foster brothers make a mockery of worship at the temple. But Samuel remained uncontaminated by their conduct while their dad, his mentor, barely tapped them on the hand and failed to discipline them adequately for their misdeeds. Later, elected as Israel's judge, Samuel exhorted his constituents to serve the Lord wholeheartedly; that if they put away all strange gods; if they did, God would deliver them from their enemies, the Philistines who were a constant thorn in their sides. The people obeyed, and Samuel called a revival meeting at Mizpeh. When the Children of Israel were meeting at Mizpeh, the Philistines took the opportunity to gather against them to war. God intervened supernaturally during the battle by causing a raging thunderstorm that confused the Philistines and enabled Samuel to win the battle.

In gratitude to God, Samuel set up a memorial rock that he called *Ebenezer*, which meant, "Hitherto has the Lord helped us." As a result of that victory, Israel was restored all their lost cities "from Ekron, even unto Gath; and the coasts thereof...and there was peace" (1 Samuel 7).

Although Samuel displayed brilliant leadership with that battle, his constituents were not impressed enough to reward him with honor. As righteous and successful as he was, they had their own agenda. They were embarrassed at being led by a priest judge instead of a king like the Philistines had. They also had issues with the character of Samuel's sons, Joel and Abijah, whom he placed as judges in the city of Beer-sheba as he himself grew older. The young men took bribes, were material minded, and "perverted judgment" (1 Samuel 8:3).

The elders formed a committee, therefore, to confront Samuel about the social deterioration that was taking place in Israel; however, while their concern was justified, their motive was entirely wrong. They went to his judgment office in Ramah where he lived and presented their complaints. "You are getting old, and your sons are out of control," they told Samuel. "They don't have the same values as you have. Make us a king to judge us like all the nations," they demanded, revealing their true motive--national envy. [People won't be happy with you or for you when their eyes are on the grass next door, especially if it looks greener. Nothing you do would be right or satisfactory to them.] The elders used Samuel's age and his sons' misbehavior as a rationale for wanting to upscale their self-esteem without weighing the consequences of their choice.

Just imagine being confronted by a team of objectors to your leadership with a daring proposal to unseat you! Samuel was unhappy, feeling rejected, of course, but he did not get angry. Instead, he took the 'vote of no confidence' to the Lord.

God shared with Samuel the proper perspective of what the elders were doing; it was a spiritual conflict that wasn't really about Samuel. God explained that:
- They rejected God and not him (Samuel);
- They did not want God's lordship;
- Give them their desire;
- Also, warn them seriously about the consequences of their choice.

The consequences would be:

- Whomever they chose would make their sons serve him and his chariots;
- Their sons would become his horsemen;
- Their king would send them to war as contingency leaders;
- They would work his fields;
- They would have to invent war instruments [God used nature instead];
- The king would use their daughters as cooks and bakers;
- The king would take the best of their farms and award them as trophies to his servants;
- The king would demand the same ten percent God asked for as His servants' rewards;
- The king would put their men, women, and cattle to work for him;
- He would demand one-tenth of their herd and make them his servants;
- He would lead them to pray to God with tears, but God will then block out their cries.

Samuel expressed these consequences to the people, but they refused to be forewarned. "It doesn't matter!" they responded. "We still want a king to reign over us. We want to be like other nations. He will judge us, and when we go out to battle, people will see our king in the lead. He will fight our battles."

Samuel told the Lord what they responded to his message.

God said to him, "Give them their choice. Make them a king!" [How many regrets we incur when we insist on having our desires over God's!]

CHAPTER TWO

THE PEOPLE'S CHOICE

There was in the tribe of Benjamin, a very important man named *Kish*. Kish had a son named *Saul*. Saul was outstanding--the most handsome man in all Israel and the tallest. You could not miss Saul in a crowd, so stunning he was! One day Kish sent Saul to search for his donkeys which had strayed away. Kish told Saul to take a servant with him.

Saul roamed the countryside looking for the donkeys. He searched town after town--Ephraim, Shalisha, Shalim, and even the town of the Benjaminites, his home. He couldn't find the donkeys. He finally reached as far as the territory of Zuph where he called it quits and told the servant that they should return home lest his father would begin worrying about them instead of the donkeys.

The servant then informed Saul that he knew of a trusted prophet who was honorable and had a 100 percent prediction record for accuracy. "How about if we pay him a visit?" he suggested.

Saul, replied, "We can go, but if we do, what shall we present to him for his counsel? We don't have a thing! Not even some bread!" [It was typical of Bible folk to erect altars to God after victories, present offerings to God after being blessed, and as in this case, to pay people for favors].

The servant replied, "I have some silver that I can pay him to tell us our way."

"Okay," Saul replied, "Let's go!"

So they went to find Samuel. On the way to the city, they ran into a group of young ladies who were going to fetch water.

"Is the prophet around?" they asked the ladies.

"A-ha!" They answered.

> He is just ahead of you. Hurry! He came only today to offer sacrifices for the people in the high place. As soon as you arrive in the city you will find him before he goes up to the high place to eat. The people are there waiting for him to bless the sacrifice. Only then will they eat what they should. Hurry! Hurry! Because you have just enough time to find him!

Just as the young ladies said, Saul and his servant found Priest Samuel going up to the high place. God had prepared Samuel by downloading into his ears the previous day that the Benjaminite he would meet the following day was to be anointed by him as captain over Israel. God added that Saul's mission was to save His people out of the hand of the Philistines because Israel's cries had gone up to Him. [How amazing it is that even when our lives are out of synch with God's perfect will, He still permits our free will to choose our destiny and He stands beside us when the going gets tough if we let Him! Also, knowing that we would ultimately fail or reject Him, He still tolerates our manipulations!]

Samuel saw this outstandingly strikingly handsome young man approaching him. At the same time, God streamed into his awareness a gift of knowledge. "Behold the man whom I spoke to you about! This same shall reign over my people" (9:14).

Saul had no such gift! He approached Samuel and asked him, "Can you please tell me where the seer is?" Saul was not only carrying around his dad's concern but he was also courteous with people.

CHAPTER THREE

A PROPHETIC ANOINTING

Samuel replied, "I am the seer; go on to the high place ahead of me because you will dine with me today and tomorrow I will let you leave and will tell you all about the dreams in your heart." [Don't you know that God knows the longings of your heart? People must have been throwing king-talk at Saul because of his good looks since he was a child, nurturing in him the dream to become a king. The prophetic word flushed it out.] Samuel continued: "And the donkeys that you are searching for? Don't worry about them--they were found. And who comes to the mind of all Israel? Is it not you and your father's family?"

Saul understood exactly what the prophet was talking about. Humility engulfed him. "Am I not a Benjaminite, the smallest of the tribes of Israel? Isn't my family the least in that tribe? Why are you talking to me like this?"

Samuel escorted Saul and his servant into the parlor and seated them in the chiefest among the thirty seats for the parlor invitees. He instructed the cook to bring the special portion of food he had previously arranged with the cook to set aside--the shoulder. He told Saul, "Go ahead and eat. I especially kept it for you for this occasion."

Samuel communicated confidentially that day with Saul. Early next day he called Saul to the penthouse, telling him that it was time for him to leave. Then he walked Saul out to the city limits where he told Saul to dismiss his servant for a while so he could tell him privately the message God gave him. After the servant left, Samuel took a vial of oil and poured it on Saul's head, and kissed him. With a deep respect for Samuel's integrity, we observe how he did not in the slightest degree diminish from the instructions God gave him for the younger man whom he knew would soon replace his authority. He said to Saul, "I'm doing this because God has anointed you to be captain over his inheritance." [Samuel had sons in the waiting!] Then Samuel told Saul where to go, whom he'll meet, what to do, and where to stay.

Things happened just as Samuel predicted. Before it all ended, Saul was transformed into an anointed man of God. When he arrived home, his uncle asked him where he had been.

"We went searching for the donkeys, and when we didn't find them anywhere, we ran into Samuel on the way home."

"No kidding!" his uncle exclaimed. "What did Samuel say to you, Boy?"

"Oh, he told us that the donkeys were found," Saul replied, wisely revealing not a word about how Samuel anointed him to be Israel's king.

CHAPTER FOUR

SAMUEL SHOWS GREAT GRACE

Now it came time for Samuel to be tested further. He called the people to Mispeh, the religious center and addressed them:

> This is what the Lord God of Israel says to you: I brought you out of Egypt, and delivered you out of the hand of the Egyptians, and out of the hand of all kingdoms, and of all your oppressors.

> Today you have rejected your God, who Himself saved you out of all your adversities and tribulations, and you have said unto Him, 'No! But set a king over us.' Now, therefore, present yourselves before the Lord by your tribes, and by your thousands.

Samuel inspected each tribe and cast lots and the tribe of Benjamin was selected. Bible protocol required two witnesses at minimum for a decision to be established. This lot, therefore, was a second confirmation for Saul to be the king elect. Within the tribe of Benjamin, the son of Matri won the next lottery, and Saul the elegant son of Kish within that family, got selected. When they went to find Saul he was nowhere to be found. He was hiding in the military accouterments, such was his initial humility! The Lord revealed to them where he was, so they went to get him.

When he appeared, his physique was commanding! His height stood out above everyone. Saul had already known that he was chosen because he was already anointed. Now he became the authentic people's choice.

Samuel announced to the people: "Look at him whom the Lord has chosen! There is no one like him among all the people!" Samuel was demonstrating exemplary grace.

The people roared, "God save the king!"

The scribes documented the occasion and put it in the archives. Then everyone went home very satisfied that they had made the right choice.

Saul went home to Gibeah where God spoke to a band of men to support him. [It is typical of God not to totally abandon us. God is not threatened by our foibles!] There were a number of men who questioned his qualifications, and out of jealousy, they did not celebrate with him and gave him no presents, as was the protocol. Saul took note of their snobbery, but he held his tongue and did not react to their spurning.

Saul did well in the early stages of his reign. His humility was impressive as he forgave those who initially opposed him when after winning a battle against the Ammonites, the people called for their death (11:13).

CHAPTER FIVE

SAUL BEGINS HIS DESCENT DOWNWARD

Saul was doing well as king until a couple of years after his inauguration he made his first spiritual snafu--to usurp the role of the priest. The Philistines were constantly harassing the Israelites. Anticipating the constant provocation, Saul assembled an army of 3,000 men. He kept 2,000 with him in Gilgal and left 1,000 with his son Jonathan in Gibeah. What do you know? Jonathan with his 1,000 contingencies attacked a garrison in Geba and won the battle. That made the Philistines mad, so they gathered 30,000 chariots, 6,000 horsemen, and people "as numerous as the sand which is on the seashore in multitude" to attack Saul. The sheer multitude of the Philistine army struck fear in the hearts of the Israelites. They took cover in caves, thickets, rocks, high places, and pits. Some of them even crossed the river Jordan as refugees in the country of Gad and Gilead. Yet Saul's army stuck with him, trembling in fear. Saul had called for Samuel to seek an answer from the Lord.

Samuel told him to give him a week for the answer, but after seven days he had not shown up. Saul, therefore, became impatient and decided to act as a priest and do the sacrificial ceremony of seeking God's face in Samuel's place. He was no sooner finished sacrificing the burnt offering when Samuel showed up. Saul went out to greet him, but he was stumped by Samuel's greeting:

"What have you done?" Samuel asked him.

CHAPTER SIX

WRONG CHOICES!

Saul answered:

> Well, I was waiting for you, and
> you didn't keep your appointment.
> Meanwhile, the people were getting
> so afraid that they were scattering
> for safety in every direction, and the
> Philistines were building up their troops
> at Michmash. I told myself they would
> come to Gilgal next, and I have not yet
> made my supplication to God. So, I
> forced myself to offer a burnt offering.

Samuel replied:

> That wasn't a smart thing to do! That
> was not what God commanded you
> to do. Unfortunately, God planned to
> establish your kingdom forever, but
> now He has to cut it off.
>
> God has searched for a leader with a
> heart like His own and has commanded

him to be captain over His people because you have not done what He commanded you to do.

That was the beginning of the end of Saul's reign. He was the people's choice over God's. Interestingly, God went along with their plan, giving them every chance to succeed. He never abandoned them. However, He drew the line when their chosen king moved in presumption, usurping Priest Samuel's authority instead of waiting and trusting the Lord. God was at the same time protecting the authority of His Priest, Samuel. in conceding to their request for his resignation, which was basically what they were doing when they asked for a king, told them:

If you will fear the Lord and serve Him, and obey His voice, and not rebel against the commandment of the Lord, then shall both you and the king that reigns over you continue following the Lord, your God...For the Lord will not forsake His people for His great name's sake: because it has pleased the Lord to make you His people...But if you shall still do wickedly, you shall be consumed, both you and your king (1Samuel 12: 14, 22-25).

AFTERWORD

As we reflect on Saul's reign, we observe how someone who starts out with every opportunity to leave a legacy of success and honor, could end up with a disreputable destiny. Saul, with his good looks, impressive personality, and personal aspirations, failed desperately as the people's choice. Somewhere along the way he became contaminated by envy of Samuel's influence and arrogance from his kingship and pushed his button too far with God. Thus, we learn that we never know what goes on in another person's mind about us. We can only assume other people's motives by the way they act toward us, and the things they say. Fortunately, if we are serving the Lord in truth as Samuel was, He watches our backs and God 'is where the buck stops,' as in Samuel's case. He promises, "I will never leave you, nor forsake you." With that promise, we can safely and successfully negotiate the manipulations and guile that go on around us, even the wiles of the devil.

PART TWO: KING DAVID--PICKED FOR A SHEPHERD'S HEART

1 Samuel 16:4-13 (KJV)

⁴And Samuel did that which the LORD spoke, and came to Bethlehem. And the elders of the town trembled at his coming, and said, Comest thou peaceably? ⁵And he said, Peaceably: I am come to sacrifice unto the LORD: sanctify yourselves, and come with me to the sacrifice. And he sanctified Jesse and his sons and called them to the sacrifice. ⁶And it came to pass, when they were come, that he looked on Eliab, and said, Surely the LORD'S anointed is before him. ⁷But the LORD said unto Samuel, Look not on his countenance, or on the height of his stature; because I have refused him: for the LORD seeth not as man seeth; for man looketh on the outward appearance, but the LORD looketh on the heart. ⁸Then Jesse called Abinadab and made him pass before Samuel. And he said, Neither hath the LORD chosen this. ⁹Then Jesse made Shammah to pass by. And he said, Neither hath the LORD chosen this. ¹⁰Again, Jesse made seven of his sons to pass before Samuel. And Samuel said unto Jesse, The LORD hath not chosen these. ¹¹And Samuel said unto Jesse, Are here all thy children? And he said, There remaineth yet the youngest, and, behold, he keepeth the sheep. And Samuel said unto Jesse, Send and fetch him: for we will not sit down till he comes hither. ¹²And he sent and brought him in. Now he was ruddy, and withal of a beautiful countenance, and goodly to look at. And the LORD said, Arise, anoint him: for this is he. ¹³Then Samuel took the horn of oil, and anointed him in the midst of his brethren: and the Spirit of the LORD came upon David from that day forward.

CHAPTER SEVEN

BEYOND RESTORATION

Saul's career as king kept spiraling downward with him making one bad decision after another. First, he usurped the priest's authority and showed no evidence of penitence. Then he disobeyed God's instruction regarding war with the Amalekites--keeping the plunder from the war, sparing King Agag, and lying to Samuel about his activities.

He made himself so detestable to God and Samuel that Samuel eventually broke connections with him up to the point of his death. Actually, the Bible says that "the Spirit of the Lord departed from Saul, and an evil spirit from the Lord troubled him" (1 Samuel 16:14). Eventually, God had enough and told him through Samuel that "rebellion is as the sin of witchcraft and stubbornness as iniquity and idolatry. Because you have rejected the word of the Lord, he has also rejected you from being king" (15:23).

Chapter Eight

David Anointed King

God sent Samuel to Bethlehem to the family of Jesse to anoint one of his sons to be king even while Saul was the reigning monarch. This was a complicated assignment since Samuel knew he would risk death if Saul heard that he anointed someone else as king in his place. Samuel had not communicated with Saul for quite some time after confronting him about his disobedience regarding the matter of Agag, king of the Amalekites. Samuel himself had to kill Agag to fulfill God's commandment. Samuel needed a diplomatic strategy to approach Jesse's family, just in case the news went back to Saul. "How can I go?" he asked the Lord. "If Saul gets wind of it, I'll be dead meat!"

The Lord told him to visit Jesse for the purpose of going to make a sacrifice. He would later give him further instructions regarding his anointing the man He chose.

Samuel went to Bethlehem where he was greeted suspiciously by the city elders. They were intimidated by the unexpected arrival of the priest judge in their town. "Are you here for peace?" they asked him.

"I'm here for peace," Samuel answered. "I have come to sacrifice to the Lord. Purify yourselves and come with me to the sacrifice." Samuel made sure that Jesse and his sons were in attendance. He began to inspect them, listening to God's leading as to which of them was God's choice.

First came Eliab. He looked so tall and handsome! *I bet this is the one,* he thought.

But the Lord said,

> Do not look at the attractiveness of his features, or the height of his stature because I have refused him because the Lord does not see things like humans. Humans are impressed by outward appearances, but the Lord examines the heart.

Jesse called his second son next--Aminadab. "I haven't chosen him either," the Lord told Samuel. Jesse called Shammah, his third son, next. "Not this son either," came the answer to Samuel. Jesse called his next four sons.

Samuel told him, "God has not chosen these. Are all of your children here?" he asked.

"Well," said Jesse, "all are here except the youngest who is taking care of the sheep."

"Send for him," Samuel told Jesse, "because we won't sit down until he gets here."

Jesse sent for the young man, and he came in. He was gorgeous--ruddy, and handsome!

The Lord told Samuel, "Arise and anoint him. He is the one!"

Samuel took his horn of oil and anointed the youngest son in front of his older brothers. The Spirit of the Lord came upon David from that day forward. Samuel left for his home in Ramah.

The Spirit of the Lord also left Saul, opening him to be troubled by an evil spirit instead. He became so disturbed that his servants recommended that he hired a skilled harpist to play music to calm him down when the evil spirit manifested on him.

One of his servants who knew David was musically talented gave Saul David's reference. "Look I have witnessed this man. He is cunning in playing. He is a mighty valiant man, a soldier, smart, good looking, and the Lord is with him."

Saul sent to Jesse for David.

When David came, Saul looked at him and his spirit took an instant liking to him so much that he hired him to be his armor-bearer. Whenever Saul came under the influence of the evil spirit, David would play the harp and it would calm Saul down and make him feel better.

Chapter Nine

Jealousy Breeds Animosity

David continued to find favor with Saul to the point at which he and Saul's son, Johnathan, became fast friends. David excelled in honor by killing the giant Goliath, and as Saul promoted him to Army General, he exercised great wisdom as a leader. However, one day when Saul heard the women praising David in dances, singing, "Saul had slain his thousands and David his ten thousands," he became insanely jealous of David.

"They are praising him for slaying ten thousands while for me for only one thousand. He will want the kingdom next!" Saul complained. From that day he made David his enemy. The following day, when the evil spirit troubled him and David came to play for him, he threw his javelin to kill David two times. David saved himself by ducking away. Jealousy burned within Saul as he plotted different ways of having David killed. When none of his plots succeeded, he became even more afraid of David and made him his arch enemy.

Soon Saul put out a bounty on David's head. He instructed his son Johnathan to kill David, but Johnathan loved his friend and cautioned him instead and helped him to escape Saul by fleeing to Samuel in Ramah where he told Samuel about Saul's behavior toward him.

Samuel helped David to hide for a while, but the word got out that he was in Naioth in Ramah, so David had to flee again for his life. He stayed on the run from Saul for years, having different opportunities to kill Saul. But he refrained from hurting the king, telling his men who urged him to do so since the Lord had prophesied his deliverance, "The Lord forbid that I should do this thing against my master, the Lord's anointed, to stretch forth my hand against him, seeing he is the anointed of the Lord" (1 Samuel 24:6). Even while David lived a destitute life, running from Saul, God used him to fight and win many skirmishes with the Philistines. Each victory accumulated renown and honor for David.

Eventually, Saul was wounded in the battle of Mt. Gilboa. He requested his armor-bearer to kill him, but the armor-bearer wouldn't, so Saul fell on his own sword, committing suicide. His son Johnathan, David's friend, and two of his brothers Abinadab and Malchi-shua died in the battle, fighting for their father, leaving one heir to contend with David's accession to the kingdom of Israel. Ish-bosheth, the surviving heir, could not rally enough support to oppose David. Two of his captains eventually assassinated him in his bed, leaving David the sole contender for the crown.

David mourned for Saul and Jonathan his friend. Following the mourning, he asked the Lord what to do, if he should go into Judah.

The Lord told him to go.

"Which city?" he asked.

"Hebron," the Lord told him.

David relocated to Hebron where the Judeans came and inaugurated him King of Judah. Following Ish-bosheth's assassination, all the tribes of Israel also went to Hebron to ask him to be their king. They inaugurated him there at the age of thirty. He reigned for forty years total between the two principalities Judah and Israel. He made great conquests and feared the Lord. When he strayed, he repented and bore the consequences of his errors. He left a great heritage of righteousness so much that God established his kingdom forever under the lineage of Jesus Christ King of Kings. His was the blessing of leaving the choice to God.

AFTERWORD

In contrast with Saul, the people's choice who was based on a copy-cat mentality (wanting to be like other nations), charisma, and faked humility. David, God's choice, was based on his sincerity, his lack of guile, and possibly his heart of a shepherd. He was transparent with God. Can you imagine how arrogant David could have become to see his seven senior brothers rejected in the queue and himself being chosen as an afterthought, then finally being anointed in their presence? His integrity surfaced even later, as he faithfully served Saul, and when for years Saul hunted him down to kill him, he never once yielded to the temptation of assassinating his rival, although he was presented with several opportunities.

David, unlike Saul, stayed in his lane until God emancipated him. David never lost the heart of a shepherd, referring to his subjects as "these sheep" and requesting the Lord not to punish them for his indiscretion (2 Samuel 24:17). As God's choice, he left us a record of honor as the progenitor of Christ the Messiah, regardless of his several documented human impediments. God indeed chooses according to the heart.

PART THREE: ADONIJAH--PICKED SURREPTITIOUSLY

1 Kings 1: 5-10 (KJV)

⁵Then Adonijah the son of Haggith exalted himself, saying, I will be king: and he prepared him chariots and horsemen, and fifty men to run before him. ⁶And his father had not displeased him at any time in saying, Why hast thou done so? And he also was a very goodly man, and his mother bore him after Absalom. ⁷And he conferred with Joab the son of Zeruiah, and with Abiathar the priest: and they following Adonijah, helped him. ⁸But Zadok the priest, and Benaiah the son of Jehoiada, and Nathan the prophet, and Shimei, and Rei, and the mighty men which belonged to David, were not with Adonijah. ⁹And Adonijah slew sheep and oxen and fat cattle...and called all his brethren the king's sons, and all the men of Judah the king's servants. ¹⁰But Nathan the prophet, and Benaiah, and the mighty men, and Solomon his brother, he called not.

CHAPTER TEN

AN ATTEMPTED COUP D'ETAT

King David had grown old. Years of fighting battles took a great toll on his strength. He was becoming increasingly feeble and felt constantly cold as his blood circulation grew slower. What did his servants prescribe for him? A young virgin to lie next to him to keep him warm! The young lady they found was named Abishag of the Shunammite clan. She was fair-skinned and attractive and she took loving care of her king without becoming his wife.

Since Adonijah, then David's oldest living son, saw that his father had gotten somewhat senile, he took upon himself to make preparations to be king while David was yet alive. He began to prepare chariots and horsemen for his cavalry. David, either too senile to know, or too feeble to care, did not even try to oppose Adonijah, and because the young man was very handsome, the people automatically considered him eligible for the throne. He was able to convince Joab, David's army chief and Abiathar, the priest, to support him.

Adonijah proclaimed an inaugural celebration for himself to which he invited just about every very important person in David's kingdom, but he strategically excluded Nathan, the prophet, Benaiah, David's war advisor, a number of other men of rank, and most notably, Solomon, his younger brother. King David had at one time prior to his decline in health announced to the nation that Solomon was his and God's pick to inherit his kingdom. In his own words:

> The Lord God of Israel chose me before all the house of my father to be king over Israel for ever: for He hath chosen Judah to be the ruler; and of the house of Judah, the house of my father; and among the sons of my father, He liked me to make me king over all Israel. And of all my sons, (for the Lord hath given me many sons!) He hath chosen Solomon, my son, to sit upon the throne of the kingdom of the Lord over Israel. And He said unto me, Solomon thy son, he shall build my house and my courts: for I have chosen him to be my son, and I will be his father. Moreover, I will establish his kingdom forever, if he is constant to do my commandments, as at this day (2 Chronicles 28: 4-7).

It is clear that Solomon did not qualify for inheriting the throne any more than Adonijah, for neither was a firstborn. Of the twenty-plus sons that David fathered, Adonijah was fourth, and Solomon was much farther down the line. Solomon's entitlement was entirely the result of him being God's pick, a fact that Adonijah himself acknowledged (1 Kings 2:15). When God chooses to favor someone, there is no one who could block that favor. Therefore, Adonijah sought to acquire the throne surreptitiously and to make himself the people's choice. Prophet Nathan got wind of the inauguration and went as a whistleblower to Bathsheba, Solomon's mother. He asked her:

Haven't you heard that Adonijah the son of Haggith has usurped the throne and our king isn't aware of it? [Sit down, lady, and] listen to my advice: your life and your son's are in grave danger! You need to go and inform the king about what is going on. Ask him, 'Didn't you, my lord, O king, swear to me, your handmaid that Solomon, your son would reign King after you? How is it that Adonijah is now king? If you do that, I will come in right after to support you and verify what you told him.

AFTERWORD

Adonijah felt deserving of inheriting David's throne because he thought himself next in line after the death of Absalom, an older brother. Once he was crowned king, it would take a coup for Solomon to gain the throne. We observe in the text how Adonijah plotted surreptitiously to access the throne using flattery, intrigue, and secrecy. Adonijah's story is relived in the arenas of politics, employment, sports and even in family relationships every day as people crave power, recognition, and fame and snub and malign others possibly more worthy than themselves to gain power and authority. We need to remember that each of us will one day stand before the judgment seat of Christ to give an account of our deeds, whether they be good or evil (2 Corinthians 5:10).

CHAPTER ELEVEN

CONSPIRACY FOILED

Bathsheba did just as Nathan the prophet advised. She went into the king's bedroom where she noticed her aged husband to whom she had birthed two sons in the prime of his life being ministered to lovingly by the young Abishag. The Bible says she took note of Abishag but did not record any communication with her. [I do believe the ladies would understand what was going on in Bathsheba's mind.] She bowed in honor to the king.

The king asked her, "What is it that you want?"

She repeated what Nathan coached her to say, then added,

> Now, look! Adonijah has crowned himself king, and you don't even know a word about it! Don't you know he has slain oxen and fat cattle and sheep--a whole lot--and called all your sons, and Abiathar the priest and Joab the army captain, but he didn't call Solomon your servant? And you, my lord, O king, everyone in Israel is holding the breath waiting to hear you announce your successor to the throne. If you don't

make that announcement, when you go
to sleep with your fathers, he will find a
way to count us as traitors and get rid
of us!

Bathsheba hardly finished her speech when Nathan the prophet
entered. He bowed to the ground before David, then addressed him.

My lord, O king, did you give out the
word that Adonijah should take your
throne? Because he has today slain a
whole lot of oxen and sheep and called
his brothers the princes, captains of the
army, and Abiathar the priest, and they
are having a grand celebration for him,
acclaiming: "God save the king!" [What
is strange,] is that he didn't invite me,
or Zadok the priest, Benaiah son of
Jehoiada, or Solomon. Was this your
command that you kept from me, not
sharing with me who would succeed
you?

The king answered, "Call Bathsheba to me!"

Bathsheba approached the king.

He told her, "As God lives who saved me out of my afflictions, just as
I swore to you in the name of the God of Israel that Solomon would
succeed me, that's just how it will be today!"

Bathsheba bowed to the earth to David and said, "Let my lord King
David live forever!"

King David then said, "Bring in Zadok the priest, Nathan the prophet, and Benaiah, Jehoiada's son." The men went in to him.

King David was obviously not as demented as the Adonijah team thought. He gave his instructions:

> Assemble my servants and have Solomon, my son ride upon my mule and bring him down to Gihon.
>
> Let Zadok the priest and Nathan the prophet anoint him there as king over Israel. Blow the trumpet and proclaim, "God save the king!"
>
> Afterward, follow behind him here to the palace and seat him on my throne to succeed me as king. I have appointed him to be king over Israel and Judah.

Benaiah exploded: "Amen! The Lord, God of my lord says that also. As the Lord was with the king, so shall He be with Solomon, and make his reign even greater!"

So Zadok, the priest, Nathan the prophet, Benaiah the son of Jehoiada, along with the Cherethites and the Pelethites, went to get Solomon and took him to Gihon where Zadok anointed him with oil as king. They blew the trumpet and the people shouted, "God save King Solomon!" So many people assembled, and the music and tumult were so loud that the earth shook.

The noise from the inauguration reached the palace where Adonijah and his supporters were revelling. Joab heard the distinct trumpet sounds and remarked, "Sounds like the city is in an uproar!"

CHAPTER TWELVE

ADONIJAH RELENTS

Right then, in came Jonathan, Abiathar's son. Adonijah, confident in his new affinity with David's ex-priest, welcomed him gladly with flattery: "Come in; because you are a valiant man and bring good news."

Jonathan replied,

> You have got to believe this! Our lord, King David, has made Solomon king! And guess what? He sent with him Zadok, the priest, Nathan, the prophet, and Benaiah, son of Jehoiada, the Cherethites and the Pelethites and paraded him on the king's mule. Zadok anointed him king in Gihon: and they are coming up from the inauguration right now. That's the tumult you heard. Solomon is sitting on your father's throne right now! And guess what else? The king's servants went to bless David, saying, "God make Solomon's throne greater than yours! And King David bowed himself on his bed and

said, 'Blessed be the Lord God of Israel
who has given me someone to sit on my
throne today and let my eyes see it!'

When the guests at Adonijah's banquet heard Jonathan's report, they started trickling out one by one to their various destinations.

Adonijah became stricken with fear of Solomon, so he got up and headed to the temple where he grabbed hold of the horns of the altar, the place where the Children of Israel went when they needed sanctuary from retribution.

News reached Solomon that Adonijah fled for refuge in the temple; that he said, "I am afraid he will have me killed with the sword. Let him swear that he wouldn't."

Solomon answered, "Well. if he proves himself worthy of life, not a hair would fall from his head. But if not, he will die." Solomon sent for him.

Adonijah went, bowing down to his brother, the new king.

Solomon looked at him and said, "Look, Boy, go on home!"

Chapter Thirteen

David Passes on the Baton to Solomon

King David knew that his time to die was fast approaching. He called Solomon and gave him certain specific instructions:

> I am going the way that every person on earth must travel. Be strong and show yourself a man! Keep the charge of the Lord, thy God; walk in his ways; keep his statutes, commandments, judgments, and testimonies, as written by Moses so that you will prosper in everything you do regardless of where you turn. In that way, you will obligate the Lord to fulfill his promises to me when he said, "If your children take heed to their way, to walk before me in truth, with all their heart and with all their soul, there shall not fail thee a man from the throne of Israel."

Then King David outlined a number of revenge tasks for Solomon to accomplish. These included executing Joab for shedding innocent blood during a time of peace, and Shimei, the son of Gera, the Benjaminite who cursed him most grievously in Mahanaim. "**I** promised not to kill him; but **you** don't let him get away with it; you are a wise man and you know what to do." David told Solomon not to forget the kindness of Barzillai the Gileadite who shielded him and his army when they were on the run from Absalom, his son who was seeking to kill him. "Be kind to his sons!" David told Solomon. Then David expired, and Solomon took over the throne.

AFTERWORD

In life everyone desires to prosper, however, many 'picks' go about seeking prosperity the wrong way like Adonijah did. Our world is full of too many examples of saboteurs, manipulators, liars, deceivers, bullies, traitors, and tyrants, people who crave to excel above others without regarding the cost. David outlined for Solomon, his son, the biblical course for prosperity: "Keep the charge of the Lord, thy God; walk in his ways; keep his statutes, commandments, judgments, and testimonies." It is the appropriate instruction for any aspiring leader.

PART FOUR: SOLOMON--PICKED FOR A CHILDLIKE HEART

1 Kings 3: 5-10 (KJV)

⁵*In Gibeon the Lord appeared to Solomon in a dream by night: And God said, Ask what I shall give thee.* ⁶*And Solomon said, Thou hast shewed unto thy servant David my father great mercy, according as he walked before thee in truth, and in righteousness, and uprightness of heart with thee; and thou hast kept for him this great kindness, that thou hast given him a son to sit on his throne, as it is this day.* ⁷*And now, O Lord my God, thou hast made thy servant king instead of David my father: and I am but a little child: I know not how to go out or to come in.* ⁸*And thy servant is in the midst of thy people which thou hast chosen, a great people that cannot be numbered nor counted for multitude.* ⁹*Give, therefore, thy servant an understanding heart to judge thy people, that I may understand between good and bad: for who is able to judge this thy so great a people?* ¹⁰*And the speech pleased the Lord, that Solomon had asked this thing.*

CHAPTER FOURTEEN

SOLOMON REIGNS AS KING

Adonijah was doing fine until one day he approached the Queen Mother with an unusual request. "Did you come to see me for peace?" Bathsheba asked.

He replied, "For peace. I've got something to ask you."
"Say on," Bathsheba responded.

> Well, you know that the kingdom was mine and that I was the people's choice to become king. However, as things happened, it has become my brother's because God picked him to have it. So now I have one little request from you; please don't say no.

"Go ahead!" Bathsheba replied. Make your request."

Adonijah, so encouraged, continued, "Speak gently to Solomon, the king, [because I'm sure he won't deny you], that he gives me King David's chambermaid to marry."

Bathsheba answered, "Well, let me talk to the king about it for you." She kept her word and went to King Solomon to present his request.

King Solomon saw his mother approaching and bowed to her reverently and then sat down on his throne. He commanded his servants to place a seat next to his throne on his right hand for her.

Bathsheba got seated and then said, "I have a small request to ask of you. Please don't deny it."

The king replied, "Ask, my mother. I won't deny you!" He prejudged himself.

She replied, "Let Abishag the Shunammite be given to Adonijah, your brother to be his wife."

King Solomon answered his mother:

> Why would you even ask me such a thing as for Adonijah to marry Abishag? You might as well ask me to let him have the kingdom also since he is my older brother. You might as well also ask for Abiathar to be priest and Joab, son of Zeruiah to keep his position! I declare that Adonijah has gone too far. He will lose his life! As God lives who has established me and set me upon David, my father's throne as he promised, Adonijah shall be executed for this today!

The king then ordered Benaiah to execute him, which he did. Then the king ordered Abiathar to go home to his farm. He told him he was worthy of death, but he would be spared because he bore the ark of the covenant of the Lord and was a man of God to his father David, enduring many of his torments, but he would no longer be a priest to the king. Solomon also took revenge on Joab, who, hearing that he was a wanted man, fled to the temple and held on to the horns of the altar. Solomon sent Benaiah after him and told him to execute him.

When Benaiah found Joab clinging to the sanctuary he ordered him to come out upon order of the king.

Joab replied, "No, I'll die here!" He knew that it was sacrilegious for him to be killed in the sanctuary and possibly thought he would be spared.

Benaiah returned word to King Solomon that Joab said he would die there.

Solomon told Benaiah: "Do exactly what he said. And bury him. It is his reward for the innocent blood of Abner and Amasa that he shed unknowingly to my father so that we won't be held into account for them."

Benaiah did as the king ordered, and the king promoted him into Joab's position as Army captain and Zadok as priest in Abiathar's place.

Meanwhile, the king told Shimei not to leave the city limits of Jerusalem upon the penalty of death. At first, Shimei was pleased with the king's leniency, telling King Solomon that it was a good gesture and made Jerusalem his sanctuary home. However, after three years, two of his servants ran away to Gath. Shimei heard about them and saddled his donkey and left Jerusalem for Gath where he found them and returned with them to Jerusalem.

Someone snitched on Shimei telling Solomon that he had gone to Gath and returned. Solomon sent for him and asked him why he broke the order which he agreed to, saying it was good. Moreover, Solomon reminded Shimei of how he cursed David, his father, and did wickedness against him. Now David would instead be blessed and God will turn his wickedness on his own head. Instead of being cursed, he, Solomon, David's son will be blessed and his throne established "before the Lord forever" (1 Kings 2:45).

The King again sent Benaiah to work to execute Shimei. Thus his throne was established with the Adonijah team of David's haters abolished, and Solomon, God's pick was secured.

AFTERWORD

Although one of the most unlikely, Solomon was God's pick as God wove into history the plan of salvation through the house of David and ultimately the restoration of the world including the Gentiles through Jesus Christ. If you are in Christ, when God picked Solomon, He picked you!

We also learn from Adonijah's intrigues against Solomon that when God picks you for an assignment, age, culture, geography, history--nothing matters or can obstruct you. The apostle Paul tells us that if God is for us, then no one can be against us (Romans 8:31). You had best put your total trust in Jesus to help you succeed. Press on without fear or doubt. God will not desert you if you remain faithful. Distance yourself from your haters and humbly enjoy your status and accompanying resources as His pick.

PART FIVE: QUEEN VASHTI--PICKED FOR POPULARITY AND INFLUENCE

Esther 1: 1-4, 9-19 (KJV)

¹Now it came to pass in the days of Ahasuerus, (this is Ahasuerus which reigned, from India even unto Ethiopia, over a hundred and seven and twenty provinces): ²That in those days, when the king Ahasuerus sat on the throne of his kingdom, which was in Shushan the palace, ³In the third year of his reign, he made a feast unto all his princes and his servants; the power of Persia and Media, the nobles and princes of the provinces, being before him: ⁴When he shewed the riches of his glorious kingdom and the honor of his excellent majesty many days, even an hundred and fourscore days... ⁹And also Vashti the queen made a feast for the women in the royal house which belonged to king Ahasuerus. ¹⁰On the seventh day, when the heart of the king was merry with wine, he commanded Mehuman, Biztha, Harbona, Bigtha, and Abagtha, Zethar, and Carcas, the seven chamberlains that served in the presence of Ahasuerus the king, ¹¹To bring Vashti the queen before the king with the crown royal, to shew the people and the princes her beauty: for she was fair to look on... ¹²But the queen Vashti refused to come at the king's commandment by his chamberlains: therefore was the king very wroth, and his anger burned in him. ¹³Then the king said to the wise men, which knew the times, (for so was the king's manner toward all that knew law and judgment: ¹⁴And the next unto him was Carshena, Shethar, Admatha, Tarshish, Meres, Marsena, and Memucan, the seven princes of Persia and Media, which saw the king's face, and which sat the first in the kingdom); ¹⁵What shall we do unto the queen Vashti according to law, because she hath not performed the commandment of the king Ahasuerus by the chamberlains? [16]*And Memucan answered before the king and the princes, Vashti the queen hath not done wrong to the king only, but also to all the princes, and to all the people that are in all the provinces of the king Ahasuerus.* [17]*For this deed of the queen shall come abroad unto all women, so that they shall despise their husbands in their eyes, when it shall be reported, The king Ahasuerus commanded Vashti the queen to be brought in before him, but she came not.* [18]*Likewise shall the ladies of Persia and Media say this day unto all the king's princes, which have heard of the deed of the queen. Thus shall there arise too much contempt and wrath.* [19]*If it please the king, let there go a royal commandment from him, and let it be written among the laws of the Persians and the Medes, that it be not altered, that Vashti come no more before king Ahasuerus; and let the king give her royal estate unto another that is better than she.*

CHAPTER FIFTEEN

A SUDDEN DEPOSITION

If the people had supreme power, Queen Vashti would never have lost her status in Persia, now Iran, as queen and wife of Ahasuerus; indeed, if only her husband had the tenacity to recant his edict that stripped her of her position. Vashti was truly the people's choice. She was very pretty, fair-skinned, and undoubtedly, body-beautiful.

So, when the king wanted to show off the riches of his kingdom, he placed Vashti on the menu list to parade her beauty wearing the royal crown in front of his drunken cabinet. Unfortunately, to her demise, she refused to comply, something unheard of before--that one, especially a woman, should disobey the order of her husband, and most treasonous if he were the king. That was the nature of the times (v. 13). Therefore the councilmen stepped into action and condemned Vashti to be removed from royalty as a precedent to prevent women in the nation from rebelling against the authority of their husbands. "Let the king give her royal estate to another that is better than she," they advised.

That advice sounded good to the king. So, with one stroke, Vashti was no more queen, practically overnight!

The speaker for the king was a man named Memucan, who after obtaining the king's consent, sent circulars to all the provinces in the different languages, giving power to every man to rule over his house.

But time has great power to diffuse anger, and King Ahasuerus began to have longing thoughts for his gorgeous wife. He was growing remorseful at what he did to her. But the laws of the land were unchangeable and he could not recant. So, the councilors came up with a bright suggestion:

> Let the king appoint officers in all the provinces of his kingdom, that they may gather together all the fair virgins unto Shushan the palace, to the house of the women, unto the custody of Hege, the king's chamberlain, keeper of the women; and let their things for purification be given them. And let the maiden which pleases the king be queen instead of Vashti.

The decision pleased the king. He made it into a decree (2:3-4). That was the last we heard about Vashti.

AFTERWORD

Vashti's predicament is a lesson to anyone who puts confidence in the sustaining power of beauty, influence, and public support. Despite her smashing looks, her acceptance ended when she took a stand for integrity. In refusing to be paraded as a 'piece of meat' as it were, she was instantly dropped as a pariah.

Over the last few years, in our society, scores of women have formed a "Me too" generation after confessing that they were sexually harassed by men of influence who have consequently been falling like pins in a bowling alley even after long years of the alleged harassment. Whatever Vashti's reason for refusing to show off her beauty at the king's command, and she should be appropriately applauded, the deeper lesson is that there is an inherent danger in allowing ourselves to court the world's approval. When a convenient time comes around, someone more talented, more beautiful, more youthful, or more popular could replace us. Hence it would be better to direct our energies into pleasing God rather than people. We read that "Vashti came no more before the king." She was soon replaced by a younger, pretty foreigner who was in God's bigger plan of things--God's choice. Make sure your choice is God's.

PART SIX: ESTHER--PICKED TO ACCOMPLISH A MISSION

Esther 2:8-10, 3:8-10, 4:8, 13-14 (KJV)

²:⁸*So it came to pass, when the king's commandment and his decree was heard, and when many maidens were gathered together unto Shushan the palace, to the custody of Hegai, that Esther was brought also unto the king's house, to the custody of Hegai, keeper of the women. ⁹And the maiden pleased him, and she obtained kindness of him; and he speedily gave her things for purification, with such things as belonged to her, and seven maidens which were meet to be given her, out of the king's house: and he preferred her and her maids unto the best place of the house of the women. ¹⁰Esther had not shown her people nor her kindred, for Mordecai had charged her that she should not show it.*

³:⁸*And Haman said unto king Ahasuerus, There is a certain people scattered abroad and dispersed among the people in all the provinces of your kingdom; and their laws are diverse from all people; neither keep they the king's laws: therefore it is not for the king's profit to suffer them. ⁹If it pleases the king, let it be written that they be destroyed; and I will pay ten thousand talents of silver to the hands of those that have the charge of the business, to bring it into the kings' treasuries. ¹⁰And the king took his ring from his hand, and gave it unto Haman the son of Hammedatha the Agagite, the Jews' enemy.*

⁴:⁸*Also he gave the copy of the writing of the decree that was given at Shushan to destroy them, to show it to Esther, and to declare it unto her, and to charge her that she should go in unto the king, to make supplication unto him, and to make request before him for her people.*

4: 13:14 *Then Mordecai commanded to answer Esther, Think not with thyself that thou shalt escape in the kings' house, more than all the Jews. ¹⁴ For if thou altogether hold thy peace at this time, then shall there enlargement and deliverance arise to the Jews from another place; but thou and thy father's house shall be destroyed: and who knoweth whether you are come to the kingdom for such a time as this?*

Chapter Sixteen

Grooming for God's Plan

In the bigger picture of things, God was working on a plan to prevent an unexpected holocaust of the Children of Israel by a vicious enemy by the name of Haman the king's chief advisor. Thus, many times we cannot perceive with our human minds exactly what His purpose and leadings are. We see a Vashti going down, but until the plot unfolds, we are veiled to see an Esther being groomed for a bold mission to save a whole nation from extermination.

Many years before Vashti, a Jewish family was carried captive from their home in Jerusalem to Persia, today's Iran, by Nebuchadnezzar, king of Babylon. While several family members died, Mordecai survived and ended up with a good position working in Shushan, the king's palace. Mordecai raised the daughter of his deceased brother as his own child. He also was instrumental in saving the king's life from an assassination attempt. When Mordecai heard about the king's edict and the maidens started gathering for the competition, Mordecai's niece was also presented among the bevy of beautiful ladies to be inspected for selection to replace the deposed Vashti.

Hegai, the keeper of the women, was very pleased with Esther. In fact, he became partial to her, favoring her over all other contestants without realizing her Jewish heritage which Mordecai had specifically warned Esther not to reveal to anyone [Never fear when God favors you!]

Meanwhile, Mordecai monitored her progress very closely.

After twelve months of grooming and pampering for royalty, the day eventually came for Esther to be presented to the king. She passed the first and second stages. At that point, she was relegated to the care of Shaashgar, the chamberlain, to await the time when the king would call her in by name for approval. Esther had wisely followed Hegai's advice to the letter and thus obtained favor at every aspect of the inspection. That resulted in her being taken into king Ahasuerus' house. He was so enamored by her, that he crowned her queen in Vashti's place without even knowing that she was a Jewish alien.

King Ahasuerus made a great coronation banquet for the occasion. But this was only the start of Esther's mission.

Now the king had set a man named Haman as his chief of staff. In that capacity, Haman received great honor and homage and exercised much power over the people. The king had even given the command that people must give him reverence by bowing down to him on sight. But Mordecai, the Jew, refused to bow down to him. This angered Haman to the uttermost especially after people revealed to him that Mordecai was a Jew. Haman decided that he would do his best to exterminate not only Mordecai but all the Jews in the kingdom also.

He took his cause to king Ahasuerus:

> There is a certain people scattered abroad
> and dispersed among the people among
> all the provinces of your kingdom, and
> their laws are diverse from all people;
> neither keep they the king's laws:
> therefore it is not to the king's profit

to suffer them. If so, it pleases the
king, let it be written that they may be
exterminated...

Haman promised to turn in the bounty--ten thousand talents of silver--into the king's treasuries.

The king bought into the proposal. He told Haman: "The case is as good as funded! Do whatever with them as you please!" The scribes were called to write it into law which the king sealed with his ring, making the decree irrevocable, and the decree was distributed throughout all the provinces.

CHAPTER SEVENTEEN

A TIMELY SELECTION

When Mordecai obtained a copy of the decree, he tore his clothing, put on mourning garments of sackcloth with ashes, and went into the city crying out a loud wail. He went and stood before the king's gate, something that was forbidden for people dressed as he was. Also, Jews were everywhere dressed like him and wailing their sentence to death.

News about Mordecai came into the palace into Esther's ears that he was at the gate dressed for mourning. She sent out regular clothes for him to change into, but he refused them. So Esther sent a personal chamberlain, Hatach, to enquire of Mordecai why he was so dressed at the king's gate.

Mordecai explained the reason to Hatach and how Haman had promised to enrich the king's treasuries with the bounty fees. He also sent her a copy of the decree and requested that she go before the king to plead with him to save the lives of her people.

Esther listened to Hatach, then responded with what everyone knew, that nobody could approach the king unless invited by him. He will then hold out his golden scepter which must be touched on the top to indicate his approval for an audience. The penalty for breaching the protocol was death. "Moreover, " Esther wailed, "he has not called for me for a whole month!"

Mordecai had an answer for her; it was blunt:

> Don't think that you will escape because you are the queen and you are living in the king's palace. You have a unique responsibility to advocate for your people. If you don't, then their deliverance will come from some other source and you and your father's house will still be destroyed. **Who knows whether you came to the kingdom for such a time as this?**

Esther, God's choice, sent back a reply:

> Go, gather together all the Jews that are present in Shushan, and go on a fast for me, and neither eat nor drink three days, night or day: I also and my maids will fast likewise; and so, will I go in unto the king, which is not according to the law: and **if I perish, I perish!**

Mordecai went home and did as Esther asked him. She also went on the three days fast along with her maids.

Chapter Eighteen

A Bold Appearance

After three days Esther donned her royal apparel and went into the inner court of the king's palace to see if Ahasuerus would hold his scepter out to her. When he saw her, he was pleased, so he held out the golden scepter, and Esther moved toward him and touched the top of the scepter. "What is it that you want, Queen Esther?" he asked her. "It will be granted, even if it is half of my kingdom!" [His pleasure was effusive!]

Esther replied, "If it pleases you, I would like for you and Haman to attend the banquet I am holding for you today."

Ahasuerus commanded Haman to hurry and prepare to attend the banquet with him. While they drank wine, he said to Esther, "What is it that you really want? You will have it--even to the half of the kingdom!"

"Well, this is my petition," Esther replied, "If I have really found favor in your eyes, and you will grant me what I request, then you and Haman come again to the banquet I will prepare for you again tomorrow. I will then tell you what my request is."

Haman left the banquet feeling very happy at being honored to attend the banquets the queen prepared for the king and him. However, on his way out, he saw Mordecai standing in the gate of the palace.

Mordecai did not bow down to him, so he became full of anger toward Mordecai. He kept his mouth shut until he got home when he sent for his confederates and Zeresh, his wife. He boasted to them of all the favor that King Ahasuerus promoted him to and promised him. "For that matter," he continued, "I was the only person Queen Esther invited into the banquet, and she has invited me again to another banquet she is having for us tomorrow." He then spilled his indignation: "You know, for all that, I can't be content as long as I keep seeing Mordecai the Jew sitting in the palace gate."

Zeresh then intervened, "Well, why don't you build a gallows fifty cubits high, and when you meet with the king tomorrow, ask him to hang Mordecai on it; then go on your merry way!"

Haman loved the idea, so he followed it through and the gallows were erected to hang Mordecai on.

Chapter Nineteen

A Restless Night for A King

As the gatekeeper of the palace, Mordecai was in a privileged position to hear and see a lot of goings-on. He had once heard about a plot by two of the king's chamberlains, Bigthana, and Teresh, who had plotted to kill the king. He reported the plot thereby saving the king's life. On the night of the first banquet, the king felt very restless and could not sleep. He thought of reading and asked for the chronicles to be read to him. There he discovered what Mordecai had done for him. "How was he rewarded?" he asked.

"Nothing was done for him," his servants replied.

"Who is in the outer court now?" the king asked. It so happened that Haman was standing in the outer court, awaiting an entrance to the king with his request to have Mordecai hanged.

The servants told the king, "Haman is in the court."

"Allow him in," he commanded. When Haman went in he asked him, "What do you think is the most appropriate way to honor someone whom the king delights in?"

Haman immediately thought that the king was speaking about him. *Who else would he be delighted in more than myself?* So, Haman answered,

For the man whom you would like to honor, O King, bring out the royal apparel that you used to wear, and the horse you ride on, and the royal crown you wear and place it on his head.

Select one of your most noble princes to adorn him with the clothing, and put him on horseback and parade him through the streets proclaiming, "This is how the king chooses to honor the person who pleases him!"

The king told Haman, "Hurry up! Get the apparel and the horse and do as you said to Mordecai the Jew."

Haman's heart melted, but he had to obey. So he took the royal clothing and the horse and paraded Mordecai throughout the city streets proclaiming, "This is how the king honors the person in whom he delights!"

CHAPTER TWENTY

DIVINE INTERVENTION

After the parade was over, Mordecai returned to his humble position at the palace gate, while Haman went home crestfallen with his head covered to his house. There he, his friends, and his wife Zeresh went into a debate over the outcome of Mordecai's honor and what it implied for Haman. "[This is serious!] You won't prevail against him!" they predicted. Even while they were in debate, the king's servants arrived to take Haman to the banquet that Esther was having for him and the king.

Once again at the banquet, the King asked Esther, "What is your request? It will be granted unto the half of the kingdom."

This time Esther replied, "If I have truly found favor in your eyes, O King, please grant me my petition to spare my life and the lives of my people." Then, in one stroke of transparency, she revealed her true heritage at the risk of her life. "We are sold," she continued, "I and my people, to be destroyed, to be slain, and to perish. I would have kept my mouth shut if even we were being sold as slaves, although our enemy had to yield to your command."

The king asked Esther, "What are you talking about? Who is this man? Where is he who dares to presume in his heart to do this?"

Esther replied, "The adversary and enemy is this wicked Haman." She gestured toward Haman. He was trembling in his boots!

The king got up immediately, steaming with anger, and walked out into the palace garden.

Haman, then seeing the king's anger, and knowing that he had fallen out of his favor, approached Esther to beg for his life.

Esther walked away from him toward the bedroom. Haman, desperate for mercy, followed her, lying on the bed pleading for his life.

Right then, the king returned from the garden and saw Haman on the bed. "Is he going to force the queen also before me in the house?" he asked.

The servants, without waiting for an order, threw a cover over Haman's face.

Harbonah, one of the king's chamberlains, spoke up and told the king, "Right now there is a fifty cubit gallows standing in Haman's house that he constructed to hang Mordecai who saved your life, O King!"

King Ahasuerus said, "Hang him on those same gallows!"

They hanged Haman on the gallows he had built for Mordecai. The king was satisfied. On that very day, he gave Haman's property to Esther, and ordered an appointment with Mordecai, because Esther explained her relationship to him. He took a ring that he had given to Haman and gave it to Mordecai instead.

Chapter Twenty-One
Mission Successfully Completed

Esther made Mordecai the keeper over Haman's house. But her mission was unfinished. She went again to the king with tears, fell at his feet, and pleaded with him to reverse in writing the decree Haman devised to exterminate the Jews. "If you really are pleased with me," she begged, "and if it seems the right thing for you to do, please reverse the decree." [He had for the third time given her favor by holding out the golden scepter for her to touch]. She continued, "For how can I endure to see the evil that shall come unto my people? Or how can I endure to see the destruction of my kindred?"

King Ahasuerus then announced in the hearing of Esther and Mordecai:

> I have given to Esther Haman's property and he has been hanged on the gallows because he tried to exterminate the Jews. Prepare a draft decree stating whatever protections you want for the Jews in my name, and I will seal it with my ring to make it irreversible.

Since Haman's earlier decree could not be reversed, on the twenty-third day of the month of Sivan, Mordecai met with the scribes and dictated a decree that gave the Jews the right to self-defense. They could "destroy," "slay," or "cause to perish" anyone who tried to assault them, and could seize their spoils. The edict was translated into every language in the one hundred and twenty-seven provinces from India to Ethiopia, and distributed by posts who rode on horses, mules, camels, and young dromedaries (8:10). Thus, the mourning for the Jews was turned to great rejoicing. Many of the people converted to Judaism from the sheer desire to be under the no penalty for self-defense law.

The date was set for the decree to be put into effect--the thirteenth day of the twelfth month, Adar. That was the same day that Haman's decree was to take effect. The Jews were well prepared to defend themselves against their haters, many of whom still ignored the self-protection edict. The Jews killed five hundred men in the palace city of Shushan alone but they did not seize their spoils.

The king met with Esther and asked her, "The Jews have slain and destroyed five hundred men in Shushan, and have captured Haman's ten sons. There is no telling what they have done in the other provinces! Now tell me what else would satisfy you? Anything you ask will be granted!"

Esther replied, "If it pleases the king, let the decree be repeated tomorrow, and let them hang Haman's ten sons on the gallows."

The king consented and on the fourteenth day, three hundred more men were killed by the Jews. When the count came in from the other provinces, the number killed was seventy-five thousand. The following day, the fifteenth was proclaimed as a day of rest and celebration. From then on the fourteenth and fifteenth of the month of Adar was established by the Jews to celebrate Purim to honor their deliverance from Haman's edict to exterminate them.

Thus the Jews, under the reign of King Ahasuerus with Mordecai next in command and Esther being queen, enjoyed a great reprieve from harassment. Vashti could not have effected such deliverance. Esther turned out to be the better choice--God's.

AFTERWORD

It is very important to determine exactly what God's plan for us in life is. Do you know why God picked you for whatever role you are in? Esther, orphaned at a young age, adopted, and an alien, did not by any means sound like someone fit to be a queen replacement for the influential Vashti, Queen of Persia. But she did become her successor, orchestrated by God within, around, and behind the scenes, and without His name being mentioned even once in the plot. What might He be orchestrating within, around, and behind the scenes of your life incognito at this moment? As you find yourself confused and querulous about your relationship with God, just communicate your fears to Him, commit to trust Him regardless of your circumstances. Have you, like Esther, come to the point of total surrender, where the potential loss does not matter? That is the point at which victory begins to happen. Prayer and fasting will not hurt. Leave the risks with God and watch Him work out your victory. He picked you against all odds and will never abandon you.

PART SEVEN: BARABBAS--ASSUMED THE BETTER OF TWO EVILS

Mark 14:43-46 (KJV)

[43]*And immediately, while he yet spake, cometh Judas, one of the twelve, and with him a great multitude with swords and staves, from the chief priests and the scribes and the elders.* [44]*And he that betrayed him had given them a token, saying, Whomsoever I shall kiss, that same is he; take him, and lead him away safely.* [45]*And as soon as he was come, he goeth straightway to him, and saith, Master, Master; and kissed him.* [46]*And they laid their hands on him, and took him.*

Chapter Twenty-Two

A Problem of Positive Identification

God's Unlikely Pick for a Treasurer

I've got to be very careful here,
Lest I'll have to bow down in shame
When I meet those eleven disciples,
One missing--Judas Iscariot by name;
Because I'm compelled to tell the truth,
And you all know I wasn't there!
So what I must say I can't fabricate,
Only extrapolate, I fear.
The matter of essence is--how was it
The treasurer Jesus picked
Knowing for sure a betrayer he'd be,
Aware that he'd be playing tricks?
Much better choices Jesus foreknew:
Take Nathaniel, the one with no guile--
Wouldn't touch a penny, for sure he wouldn't;
No need on him to keep an eye!
Thomas--the one with a scientist's eye,
Who must see and must touch to believe--
Would have all transactions i's dotted, t's crossed,
No reason ever to think he'd deceive!
He could have picked Peter, the argumentative one,

He sure would have called out the cause
If a nickel turned up missing from the treasury bin,
Might tell John to tell Jesus, the Boss.
What of Philip and Andrew, bringers to Christ?
The charity line would be long!
And James or John who justice sought
As treasurers, they'd never go wrong.
But I've wondered and pondered time and again
Why of them all, Judas Iscariot was God's pick.
Judas talked as if thrifty, concerned for the poor,
But his opportunism exposed him as sick.
And Jesus so knowing gave him many a chance
To come clean from the betrayer's part;
And John called his number--a fake and a thief--
No genuine concern in his heart.
I've concluded that with God appearances don't count.
He examines our mission and purpose;
That He'd pick a person and give him or her a chance
To be bona fide, fair and just.
So if a betrayal has to occur as Jesus said,
Pray God that woe won't on you fall.
If God picks you for a task to achieve,
May you prove that it won't make you fall!

Have you ever wondered how Jesus could fellowship with Judas Iscariot for three years, eat with him, even wash his feet, knowing that he would eventually betray him? Although Judas's destiny was foretold by the prophets, one notices that Judas was presented a number of opportunities to choose not to betray Jesus. Judas, the insider, did not have to be the person who delivered Jesus for crucifixion. It seems as if the Lord was giving him chances to choose not to be that person. We see him in the house of Simon the leper where he ran his mouth off at Mary until Jesus had to rebuke him. He was so incensed at the honor she gave Jesus that his anger led him on a downward spiral from that time on. He opened a door to greed that he couldn't close thereon and satan entered into him. He was so provoked that he went to the chief priests and asked them for a reward to turn Jesus over to them. He covenanted for thirty pieces of silver. We need to monitor our motives closely for doing (and not doing) things. Matthew tells us that "from that time he (Judas) sought the opportunity to betray Jesus." He became a full-blown traitor, a marked assassin at heart. There was no turning back.

Let's follow the plot between Matthew and John. The day of the feast of unleavened bread came when Jesus took the opportunity to teach his disciples servant leadership by washing their feet. Judas was right there among them and got his feet washed. That was another conviction moment when his heart had to tell him that he was being disloyal to his Master. Matthew tells us that Jesus warned that someone at the table would betray him. Judas, knowing that he had already put a contract on the Lord's head, still asked, "Master, is it I?" (Matthew 26: 24-25). That was yet another opportunity for him to recant. He didn't. Judas had his feet washed, participated in the communion where Jesus said the wine represented his blood that would be shed for many, heard Jesus say that the betrayer would receive the sop, took the sop, and then deliberately alienated himself from the Jesus team. "And it was night!"

It is a tale of the backslider who chooses to alienate from fellow believers, and eventually from the Lord himself. The wages of sin is indeed death when repentance comes too late and one allows satan to have the upper hand often through petty peeves and quirks. Judas was being given the opportunity to become God's pick to spare Christ; instead, he chose to betray the Lord. Even when given several chances to repent, he chose to serve as the positive identifier and the people's pick instead. Matthew tells us that Jesus said: "The Son of man goeth as it is written of him: but woe unto that man by whom the Son of man is betrayed! it would have been good for that man if he had not been born" (Matthew 26:24). Take a look at the choice with which you are now being confronted and seize the opportunity to turn betrayal into defense. That is God's way!

Chapter Twenty-Three

His Luckiest Day

Matthew 27: 21-26 (KJV)

²¹The governor answered and said unto them, Whether of the twain will ye that I release unto you? They said, Barabbas. ²²Pilate saith unto them, What shall I do then with Jesus which is called Christ? They all say unto him, Let him be crucified. ²³And the governor said, Why, what evil hath he done? But they cried out the more, saying, Let him be crucified. ²⁴When Pilate saw that he could prevail nothing, but that rather a tumult was made, he took water, and washed his hands before the multitude, saying, I am innocent of the blood of this just person: see ye to it. ²⁵Then answered all the people, and said, His blood be on us, and on our children. ²⁶Then released he Barabbas unto them: and when he had scourged Jesus, he delivered him to be crucified.

It had to be the luckiest day of his life when Barabbas, the insurrectionist, was released from the custody of the Roman government as the people's choice over Jesus of Nazareth--self-proclaimed Messiah of the oppressed Jews. He had to be feeling like a turkey receiving the presidential pardon for Thanksgiving Day! *Could this be true?* Yes; it was. He was the people's choice for the governor's Passover Feast pardon, clamored for by the huge crowd: "Give us Barabbas! Away with Jesus!"

According to Matthew, the disciple, Pontus Pilate struggled with the fact that he could not find justifiable evidence for destroying Jesus.

Pilate seemed to go to great lengths to make Jesus incriminate himself for treason against the government, while the chief priests and elders did their best to convict him of breaking the Sabbath, Either conviction was deemed punishable with death by crucifixion.

Try as he did, Pilate was unsuccessful. He asked Jesus at first, "Are you the king of the Jews?"

"You are the one saying it," Jesus answered. How could he deny that he was?

Then the priests and elders jumped into the affray, but Jesus let them have the field, answering them not a word.

Marveling at his silence, Pilate tried again: "Do you not hear all the things they are accusing you of?"

Jesus remained silent, to Pilate's astonishment. Pilate had then to try another strategy. In his heart, he knew that the religious leaders were motivated by envy. "Whom should I release to you, Barabbas, or Jesus who is called Christ?" he pursued to ask. You could almost see his heart pumping with the hope that they would answer, *Jesus*. He was feeling pressured. He felt the need to take a seat.

Chapter Twenty-Four

Judgment Perverted

As he sat on the judgment seat, a messenger arrived with a message for him from his wife: "Don't you touch that innocent man!" she said. "I went through a lot of suffering today because of him!" But Pilate had to deal with not only the chief priests and elders but also the multitude whom they riled up. He again asked the rioters, "Which of the two do you want me to release?"

They answered: "Barabbas!"

"Then what shall I do with Jesus who is called Christ?"

The crowd shouted back, "Let him be crucified!"

"Why? What evil did he do?" Pilate asked.

They broke out into a rabble: "Let him be crucified! Let him be crucified!"

Pilate could not still the mob, so he took some water and washed his hands in their sight, saying: "I am innocent of the blood of this just man: you do it yourselves!" [Did you hear him say "just"?]

The mob answered, "Let his blood be on us and on our children!" [What a terrible thing it is to invoke judgment for your action on your children!]

Then, although he found Jesus' innocent, he released Barabbas whom the disciple Mark called a murderer, to his freedom, because "Pilate wanted to please the people" (Mark 15:7,11,15).

AFTERWORD

Barabbas was mentioned in each of the four gospels as the people's choice over Jesus. Luke's record supports Mark's by stating a sad comment that Pilate "released unto them him that for sedition and murder was cast into prison, whom they had desired; but he delivered Jesus to their will" (Luke 23:25). John calls Barabbas a robber (John 18:40).

Wikipedia, the free encyclopedia says that the name Barabbas means 'son of the father.' This is an interesting comparison with Jesus, the Son of God, the Father. It becomes more meaningful to think that Barabbas, 'son of the father' had his sentence commuted by Jesus, the Son of God. His sentence is symbolic of the freedom anyone can receive through accepting Jesus as Savior and be saved from sin, judgment to come, and the fires of hell.

PART EIGHT: JESUS OF NAZARETH-- GOD'S PERFECT LAMB--PICKED FOR SUFFERING

Matthew 27: 27-31 (KJV)

26b ...and when he had scourged Jesus, he delivered him to be crucified. 27Then the soldiers of the governor took Jesus into the common hall, and gathered unto him the whole band of soldiers. 28And they stripped him, and put on him a scarlet robe. 29And when they had platted a crown of thorns, they put it upon his head, and a reed in his right hand: and they bowed the knee before him, and mocked him, saying, Hail, King of the Jews! 30And they spit upon him, and took the reed, and smote him on the head. 31And after that they had mocked him, they took the robe off from him, and put his own raiment on him, and led him away to crucify him.

Isaiah 53:8-10 (KJV)

8He was taken from prison and from judgment: and who shall declare his generation? for he was cut off out of the land of the living: for the transgression of my people was he stricken. 9And he made his grave with the wicked, and with the rich in his death; because he had done no violence, neither was any deceit in his mouth. 10Yet it pleased the Lord to bruise him; he hath put him to grief: when thou shalt make his soul an offering for sin, he shall see his seed, he shall prolong his days, and the pleasure of the Lord shall prosper in his hand.

Chapter Twenty-Five

He Was Despised and Rejected of Men

There is no pen that can adequately write the worthiness of Jesus of Nazareth as God's pick for the salvation of humanity. There we see him at Pilate's mercy, who could with just a sentence free him. Instead, he let Barabbas go free and had Jesus whipped, and then turned him over to the soldiers to be crucified.

The soldiers acted like eagles over a carcass. First, they carried him to the common hall where they paraded him before all the soldiers. Then they disrobed him naked and dressed him in a purple robe symbolic of royalty. It was going to be a circus show! Next, they wove a crown made from thorns and stuck it on his head, and cut a reed and stuffed it into his right hand. Then they pranced around him mocking him saying, "Hail, King of the Jews!" Several spat on him, and pulled the reed out of his hand and beat him on his head with it. After they had their fill of mockery, they took the purple robe off him and put back his own clothes on him. Then they led him toward the hill where he was to be crucified.

On their way, they met a black guy, a citizen from Cyrene, whom they commanded to carry his cross.

The procession stopped at Golgotha's hill where they fixed a drink of vinegar mixed with gall for him to drink. He refused to drink it. They crucified him then cast lots as to who would keep his clothing as a souvenir. They put up a sign which read: **This is Jesus the King of the Jews.** His cross was placed between those of two thieves who were crucified on the same day. As people walked by they mocked him asking why he could not save himself since he saved others. Were there among them some people whom he healed, or fed? "If he is indeed king and Son of God, let him come down off the cross!" they jeered. Even the two thieves mocked at him, although one of them repented.

Around the ninth hour, Jesus cried out aloud to his Father, "Eli, Eli, lama sabachthani?" meaning, "My God, my God, why hast thou forsaken me?"

"He is calling for Elias, [the prophet]," some said.

Someone took a sponge, dipped it in vinegar, and gave him to drink. Others mocked saying, "Leave him alone; let's see if Elias would come to rescue him."

Jesus then cried out again loudly, "It is finished! Father, into Thy hands I commend my spirit" and then he expired.

Chapter Twenty-Six
Nature Protested

For three whole hours, the land went dark and nature protested his suffering with a massive earthquake that spilled rocks and split the veil that covered the temple from top to bottom. Graves opened up and many of the saints rose from the dead and appeared to people. These happenings caused the centurion on guard to remark, "Truly this was the Son of God!"

During the evening, one of his disciples, Joseph of Arimathea, a rich man went to ask Pilate to release the body to him. Pilate consented. So Joseph wrapped his body in clean linen and laid it in his own tomb which he had hewn for himself. He placed a huge stone in front of the entrance, then left.

The following day, the chief priests and Pharisees formed a council that went to ask Pilate permission to secure the entrance. "We remember how the deceiver said that he would rise again after three days. We don't want his disciples to steal his body and then claim that he rose from the dead. That would only make things worse."

So, Pilate gave them permission to seal the tomb and provided a watchman to guard it.

AFTERWORD

As we follow the proceedings surrounding the crucifixion of Jesus, we can hear the voice of the prophet Isaiah telling us decades before what God's choice for Messiah would have to endure. Being God's choice does not immunize you from persecution. In fact, it might draw persecution to you, as it did Jesus. While Barabbas was guilty of his crimes, Jesus of Nazareth "did no violence, neither was any deceit found in his mouth" (Isaiah 53:9). While Barabbas was embraced, Jesus was "despised and rejected of men...oppressed and afflicted...taken from prison and from judgment..." Why was Jesus The Father's perfect pick? Couldn't there be another person or way to redeem humans after Adam messed up? What was unique about Jesus as God's pick? Why was there the need for choosing a redeemer, in the first place?

Revelations gives us the answer (12:7-12). There John tells us that there was war in heaven. The archangel Michael battled against satan and the angels that were his charges. Satan was defeated and cast out of heaven to the earth where he has been raging war against the followers of God who "have the testimony of Jesus Christ" (v.17) to whom God gave the earth (under the lordship of Adam, Genesis 1:26-28).

Through disobedience, Adam, yielding to Eve, his wife, gave precedence to satan's instructions over God's. That gave satan the legal right to become lord over Adam and his heirs. An intervention plan had to be instituted if God was to regain sovereignty over the earth and save humanity from eternal separation from God. In the Garden of Eden, God slew animals to cover the original pair from their nakedness which was manifested after they sinned. But what of the rest of the world? It was necessary for someone to become the sacrificial lamb to make everyone eligible for redemption.

Chapter Twenty-Seven

He Is not Dead. He Is Risen!

On the third day after the crucifixion, two ladies went early in the morning to check the sepulcher out. Another great earthquake occurred because the angel of the Lord appeared and rolled back the stone that had sealed the door to the sepulcher and sat on the stone. The angel's face was all light and his clothing was as white as snow.

The watchmen saw the angel and became frightened to death.

The angel spoke to the women and said, "Do not be afraid. I know why you are here. You are looking for Jesus who was crucified. He is not here. Come take a look and see where his body was. He is risen!"

Afterword

Prior to the coming of Jesus of Nazareth, priests, who acted as intercessors for humanity, used the blood of specified animals, their lives for people's lives, as a symbolic ritual for redemption. But until Jesus, who could become the justified redeemer? Two-thirds of the angels in heaven stood loyal to God, the Father when satan rebelled through envy (Ezekiel 28:13-18). Yet none of them could be eligible since a contingency of them evidenced their capability of disloyalty to God, that is, sinning.

Great as the revered patriarchs were--Abraham, Isaac, Moses, and so on, even faithful Enoch whose walk with God earned him instantaneous translation, none could qualify to be the Redeemer. The Redeemer had to meet certain requirements that only Jesus of Nazareth could meet.

The Redeemer had to be willing, divine, human, perfect and approved by God. God could have justifiably abandoned Adam's descendants to eternal separation from Him, but thankfully, Jesus rose up to the plate in Psalms 40:6-8, interpreted by the writer of Hebrews 10:5-10:

> Wherefore when he cometh into the world, he saith, Sacrifice and offering thou wouldest not, but a body hast thou prepared me. In burnt offerings and sacrifices for sin thou hast no pleasure. Then said I, Lo, I come (in the volume of the book it is written of me,) to do Thy will, O God. Above when he said, Sacrifice and offering and burnt offerings and offering for sin thou wouldest not, neither hadst pleasure therein; which are offered by the law; Then said he, Lo, I come to do thy will, O, God. He taketh away the first, that he may establish the second. By the which will, we are sanctified through the offering of the body of Jesus Christ once for all.

The one chosen had to be willing. Jesus was indeed willing as seen in his prayer in the garden, "Not my will but Thine be done."

The chosen one had to be human as well as divine. His humanity gave him the right to represent us as earthlings. The blood of animals instituted under the law of Moses was a mere shadow of the need for a permanent and totally inclusive sacrifice. The writer of Hebrews tells us about the efficacy of Jesus's blood:

> ...neither by the blood of goats and calves, but by his own blood he entered once into the holy place, having obtained eternal redemption for us" (Hebrews 9:12, 14).

Jesus explains the efficacy by saying, "For this is my blood of the New Testament, which is shed for many for the remission of sins" (Matthew 26:28).

How then could the divine Son of God become human thereby fulfilling the legal protocol for representing earthlings? Galatians tells us that "when the fullness of the time was come, God sent forth His Son, made of a woman, made under the law to redeem them that were under the law, that we might receive the adoption of sons" (Galatians 4: 4,5).

His divinity established a connection between the Creator and his creation, providing representation for humans both in heaven and on the earth.

The chosen one had to be perfect--sinless. Even angels have been known to sin, that is, to act contrary to God's will. Jesus was always submissive to the Father's will. He said, "I and the Father are one." Jesus passed the test of perfection. Peter verified this when he said:

> ...you were not redeemed with corruptible things, like silver or gold, from your aimless conduct received by tradition from your fathers, but with the precious blood of Christ, as of a lamb without blemish and without

spot. He indeed was foreordained before the foundation of the world, but was manifest in these last times for you who through Him believe in God, who raised Him from the dead and gave Him glory, so that your faith and hope are in God (1 Peter 1:17-21).

Finally, Jesus had to meet the criterion of God's approval. That was evidenced when John the Baptist greeted him with, "Behold the Lamb of God, which taketh away the sin of the world" (John 1:29) and when, after Jesus was baptized, a voice came from heaven saying, "This is My beloved Son, in whom I am well pleased" (Matthew 3:17, Mark 1:11, Luke 3: 21-24, and John 1:30-34). Also, Jesus received heavenly approbation when at his transfiguration a voice spoke out of a cloud saying, "This is My beloved Son in whom I am well pleased; hear ye him" (Matthew 17:5), or, put into Luke's mouth, "This is my beloved Son: hear him" (Luke 9: 35).

Jesus again received his Father's approbation after Phillip and Andrew told him about the Greeks' inquiry of him, Jesus reported that his soul was troubled. In a brief gasping prayer, he said, "Father, glorify Thy name." The responding God answered from heaven, "I have both glorified it, and will glorify it again" (John 12:28).

PART NINE: IF GOD PICKED YOU

John 15:16 (KJV)

You have not chosen me, but I have chosen you, and ordained you, that you should go and bring forth fruit, and that your fruit should remain: that whatsoever you shall ask the Father in my name, He may give it you.

Chapter Twenty-Eight

If God Picked You

Jesus made it clear in the preceding scripture that his picks are intentional. They also come with waivers for success and longevity. *Yeah!* you say, *Until almost all of them had their heads cut off! That was how long!* But I am sure that if you could ask any one of his disciples now if their lives were worth it, they would tell you *Yes!* Jesus wanted them and us to know that once we enlist with him, we could be guaranteed support from the Father's end. Persecutions may arise from our end, but He is ever near us and will ensure our empowerment to overcome whatever the devil might try to use to discourage us. When Jesus walked the shores of Galilee, picking men from the fishing community to become martyrs for our salvation, it was, like he said, deliberate, not by convenience or chance, and it turned out well to the benefit of millions who have accepted Him as their Savior. Now, what about you? What were you deliberately picked for?

If God picked you for an assignment, there are many pieces of evidence from our gallery of picks of why He picked you and not someone else-- not your older sibling; not your prettier or more attractive neighbor; not your wily or more articulate friend; not your more intelligent classmate; not your charismatic competitor. Among the several reasons He may have picked you might be found one of the following:

a)   Like David, you had a shepherd's heart. While David toiled with the sheep, God was grooming him to lead Israel in safe pastures; to be resilient--not to give up on people just because they would not do right; not to give in to frustration when they wouldn't listen to sane advice; not to be impulsively revengeful. He had to learn how to use both the rod and the staff to comfort the sheep; not to run off on vacations and leave the sheep prey to malicious or aspiring intruders; not to overwork the sheep but to know when to lead them beside still waters of restoration; how to model for them righteous judgment; how to stand at the door and call them by name and dare any wolf to attack them; how to go seeking the one stubborn lost sheep who would not abide in the fold; how to be there for them in troubled times of sickness, divorce, when their children rebel, or when a loved one dies, or hardest--when your love and caring is spurned. If God picked you, you need to learn how to prepare a table for your sheep right when their enemies are watching them, smirking, expecting them to starve or fail; how to anoint them with the oil of approval so liberally that their cup runs over with appreciation for God's goodness, mercy, and grace. You will never hear David say, "I don't have the time or patience for their folly!" Who are the sheep to whom God has assigned you? Do you have a shepherd's heart, or that of a hireling? Go ahead and show it!

b)   If God picked you, He must have seen in you a heart like that of Solomon--the humble heart of a little child (1 Kings 3:7) regardless of the fact that people misjudge you--who when slighted by Adonijah, his brother, gave him space to redeem himself. Solomon applied his heart unto wisdom and in so doing, obtained unprecedented riches and honor (v. 13) that he did not even ask for. The position you are in today is good evidence that you were picked by God for your assignment which, like Solomon, only He can enable you to navigate because of your childish mentality or even like him, your tie to the flesh. Note how God's picks do not come in perfect wrappings. You, like Solomon, might have your foibles, yet if God picked you in spite of them, it

80

was a setup. He intended for you to accomplish your mission and will empower you to do it, if you ask him.

c)   If God picked you, like He picked Esther, it was to have someone most unlikely who would follow godly advice to intercept the holocaust of his people, whoever they are. It could be a project, a church, or a defenceless person. You may not have the beauty, resources, or influence of your competition but you have all you need--humility, loyalty to your heritage, obedience, faith, and daring. Those are enough to overthrow people deemed worthier than you. You may even be an alien. Yes, God uses aliens if needed. So, whoever you are, obey him and his purposes will be accomplished with credit to you, much as your haters wouldn't acknowledge it. Don't be surprised when their schemes backfire as Haman's did!

d)   If God picked you like others not mentioned in our gallery of picks, for example, Joseph, He intends to use you to save lives in the future, perhaps at the cost of surrendering your rights to your father's favor, your brothers' affection and justice, or your employer's trust. Or like the minor prophet Habakkuk, who at first could not comprehend how a pure and holy God would open his (Habakkuk's) eyes to rampant injustice and remain silent. Still, Habakkuk chose to stand on his watchtower and wait for God's time to act, declaring that though abject poverty, famine, and lack prevailed, yet he would rejoice in and acknowledge God as his salvation (Habakkuk 1:3; 2:1; 3:17-19). You must remain faithful regardless of the several months or years of injustices life throws at you, and hold on until your change comes, as it will.

e)   Or perhaps, like Saul of Tarsus who had to walk away from the establishment of apostles for three years to establish renown first in Arabia. He subsequently returned to consult with Peter over two weeks before he would receive acceptance as a leader and become the pioneer who took the Gospel to the Gentiles under the name of *Paul* (Galatians

1:18-24). Ignore the lack of human recognition and do your services to the Lord, and not to men. Yes, to some you may look like a fool, helping to make others more successful than yourself, like Paul did. Your heavenly reward will be awesome!

f)   Or Mark, whom Paul rejected temporarily on account of one discrepancy but was eventually recognized as being important to the Gospel by him later (Acts 15:37-38; 2 Timothy 4:11).

g)   If God picked you over a people-favored Barabbas, it is because you are marked to become a savior to many who would dare to vouch for you against the rabble. You might well be God's sacrificial lamb of redemption for people He marked for his kingdom. The position you hold was not given to you because you were popular, creditable, or wicked. Jesus was not any of those. He was despised, rejected by men, and thought smitten of God according to the prophet Isaiah. Is that you? Aah! But that 'sheep before his shearers' was the very Lamb of God who was to take away the sins of the entire world--whoever would allow him! Stay focused on your mission and let God work his purposes in you.

Moses, who knew God face-to-face, gives us an accurate description of God's mind as He engages in the process of selection. It is found in Deuteronomy 7:7-10:

i)   He chose you because you were different from other people. Does that sound familiar about you? Do people think or say this to you? The Israelites were chosen from all other nations because they were holy unto the Lord. Do you find yourself accused of being too holy? That's it--you are chosen by God! (Deuteronomy 7: 6).

ii)   He chose you not because you were the majority, but were loved by God; fewer than other nations, and living in a covenant relationship with God, perhaps through a dedication vow between your foreparents and God. Many Israelites are walking today who are not slightly aware that they are a people of covenant. So are many Gentiles who do not even realize that their parents dedicated them as babies to God and He has obligated himself to keep his covenant to make them his own (Deuteronomy 7: 7- 8). Pick opportune times to remind your children that they were marked for (dedicated to) God, and as such, they are expected to be different--special--blessed, if they live by God's rules.

iii)   God keeps his covenants of redemption to a thousand generations (v. 9). That is a long time to count! And He is still counting up mercy and love to Abraham's seed by birth and adoption through Christ. That's why He picked you! (Deuteronomy 7: 9).

iv)   God repays those who hate him. He is to be revered! (Deuteronomy 7:10).

The bottom line is, if you are God's pick, there is no way you can fail if you are obedient to his words. He puts the whole army of heaven at your disposal to defend, honor, and favor you. If He is for you, no man can stand against you (Romans 8:31). He watches over you with love, to the destruction of your enemies. You should now be able to affirm Zephaniah 3:17: "The Lord thy God in the midst of thee is mighty; he will save, he will rejoice over thee with joy; he will rest in his love, he will joy over thee with singing." Have you ever sung to God? Well, don't you know that if you are his pick, he sings over you?

v)   If God picked you, "Fear thou not...Let not your hands be slack" (v. 16)!

ADDENDUM

Human life is composed of sequences of choices from birth to the time we take our final breath. Those choices can bring us much satisfaction or be the source of deep sorrow or regrets. The degree to which we experience joy depends upon whether or not we learn to choose like God chooses, using eyes that discern what is most important in any given person or situation. Superficial choices tend to bring us regrets. We need to learn to go beyond the appearance and investigate what motivates the heart--as with David--lack of guile, compassion, patience; or as with Esther--tenacity, faith, commitment; or as with Our Lord--empathy, lack of retribution, loyalty to God, and love for the diminutized and lost. We are facing visible as well as invisible foes daily who do not mean us well. Yet, those who are believers in Christ know that he has their backs and will never leave nor forsake us. We are winners. Satan is a loser who is recruiting followers to populate hell because we have a choice and he and his acolytes don't.

It is encouraging later to know that Jesus gave us the key to God's kingdom and by accepting him, we are on the winning side, no matter what the devil throws at us. So let us pick like God picks--with discernment. In closing, let me share a personal experience that alerted me to the darker side of life and cautioned me to be aware of how important it is to learn to pick with discernment.

In my teaching career, I was once assigned an extremely disruptive class of students. It seemed as if I was deliberately picked on to have students who were out-of-control. There was one particular young lady who challenged my years of teaching experience, my intervention skills, my book knowledge, and reputation for being an effective teacher. [I really do believe that Christians are often picked on because of their testimony for Christ. Because Christian workers strive to live by the Matthew 5 principles, non-believers tend to take advantage of their accommodating persona and often give them the dirtier end of the stick. Thus, the devil targets them to make their lives as miserable as they let him, especially since he knows that teachers, for example, are not allowed to use the defensive weapon of prayer with disruptive students and are not to engage in religious interactions with them].

On one very frustrating day, after trying every technique I knew with this young lady I muttered under my breath thinking that I was inaudible, "Satan, in the name of Jesus, I rebuke you!"

To my astonishment, she instantly responded, "You remember what I did to him, don't you?"

The age and level of the intellectual development of the primary grade student did not match that response, hence, in my shock to hear her answer, I was prepared to do battle, but I wanted first to be sure that what I thought I heard was correct. So, I queried, "What did you just say?"

She immediately became sheepish and mumbled something like, "Never mind!" But I had already gotten an unexpected glimpse of Satan's dark side manifested in an innocent child that has become an unforgettable memory for me. Unfortunately, her backing down robbed me of the retort I intended to tell her: "And you do remember what happened three days after, don't you?"

Daily life interactions may appear simple, but in reality, may hold deeper and more complicated meanings that can influence the choices we make. We need the on-going inspiration of the Holy Spirit to give us God's discernment to make wise decisions.

If Jesus was still bones or ashes in a tomb on Calvary, believers couldn't walk around with confidence that to believe and choose him is to make the correct choice for our lives. God's choice never ends in defeat, regardless of the intervening circumstances. Jesus, God's gift to the world, rose from the dead, was seen of his disciples and many others, and over the two thousand years plus since, has been reported by thousands whose lives have been positively changed as a result of an encounter with him. He told Judas, his disciple, "If a man loves me, he will keep my words: and my Father will love him, and we will come to him, and make our abode with him" (John 14:23). That means he is the accessible and approachable pick of God for our salvation.

Today, if your mind is scrambling for an answer regarding the reality that one can find in Jesus, try talking to him yourself. Ask him to reveal himself to you. He will. Then serve him with all your heart, soul, and spirit, and plan to spend eternity with him in his joyous forevermore. He will be the best pick you will ever make. Blessings!

Thank you for reading my book. Did you enjoy it? If so, I will appreciate it very much if you would leave me a review at your favorite retailer.
Thanks!

-Norma Evans Barber

ABOUT THE AUTHOR

Norma Evans Barber is a retired teacher who spends most of her days reading and writing. She has been a teacher for most of her life in the fields of elementary education, special education and Bible studies in and around the Metropolitan District of Columbia community. Her writings are done with the objective of putting faces on Bible characters to encourage Bible literacy through meaningful life connections.

She conducted the Bread of Life International Fellowship in Washington DC and the workshop, "The Masks We Wear" for hurting women. Norma is married and has a young adult daughter. She holds a Bachelor's and Master of Education degree from Howard University and a Certificate of Graduate Studies from Regent University.

Discover Other Titles by Norma Evans Barber

Helping you see the faces as you read the Bible
Children of the Promise
Children of the New Covenant
Princess Tamar's Tears
He Spoke in Red (In Progress)

Autobiography in Poetry
Pulse Beats

Connect with Me:
Facebook: facebook.com
Twitter: https//twitter.com/NobarNorma?edit=true
Linkedin: https://linkedin.com/in/norma-barber-b7412552

Blessings!

1 Corinthians 1: 26-29 (KJV)

[26]For you see your calling, brethren, how that not many wise men after the flesh, not many mighty, not many noble, are called.

[27]But God hath chosen the foolish things of the world to confound the wise; and God hath chosen the weak things of the world to confound the things which are mighty; [28]And the base things of the world, and things which are despised, hath God chosen, yea, and things which are not, to bring to naught things that are: [29]That no flesh should glory in His presence.

www.ingramcontent.com/pod-product-compliance
Lightning Source LLC
Chambersburg PA
CBHW070438130626
46553CB00006B/2240